A FRESH
RESTART

A FRESH
RESTART

"MY COLLECTION OF POETRY & WORKBOOK"
OVER 50 TRUE STORY POEMS

PEDRO **LEBRON**

A FRESH RESTART
OVER 50 TRUE STORY POEMS

iUniverse books may be ordered through booksellers or by contacting:

iUniverse
1663 Liberty Drive
Bloomington, IN 47403
www.iuniverse.com
844-349-9409

ISBN: 978-1-6632-1067-8 (sc)
ISBN: 978-1-6632-1068-5 (e)

Print information available on the last page.

iUniverse rev. date: 10/23/2020

Contents

Spanish Poems

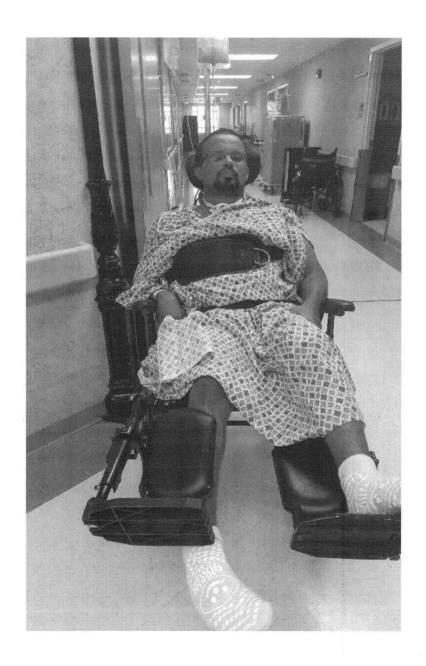

Intro

I recently suffered a Traumatic Brain Injury. My life was forced to reset. I went from living in a 5-bedroom home with a live-in maid, and my wife did not work. I owned three companies with over 160 Employees. Drove a $90,000 BMW, owned three motorcycles including the Harley I was forced to crash in. I had my accident and ended up living in my little sister's guest room with my wife, two kids and even the dog. All in one room. Now just for the record, I just want to remind you that material things don't matter, just trying to give you an idea of the drastic changes. Normal time of recovery for a TBI (Traumatic Brain Injury) patient is five years minimum. I am currently on my third year. Still recovering and working hard to continue to be a provider for my family and get my life back in order.

I am definitely not the same person. Trust me, you would not be either if you would go thru what I went thru. One of the different things I am doing now is writing poetry. I have written Poems for girlfriend and things like that in the past, but never a book of Poems. Every poem in this book is completely written with my pure reality and 100% honesty. They are all applicable to my new life now. Something in my entire life I never thought I would be doing. I have expressed my most honest feelings in this book, but I have also provided some space for you to try and do the same. Read the tittle of each poem. Next you will find the space to create your own. Try to place yourself in that tittle / situation or similar and/or create your own poem with your own tittle. Email me your creation if you want to share. The winner of all poems submitted will be publicize on my next book.

Fox example: On this first poem on page 10, I wrote Reborn at 36, because I died and came back to life at age 36 at time of accident. If you were to be reborn. At what age do you imagine that would be? Also, what do you think you will be doing? There is a space next to each poem for you to write your own. As for the other ones, what would you say on a poem with a tittle like the one or similar to the one you are looking at?

.

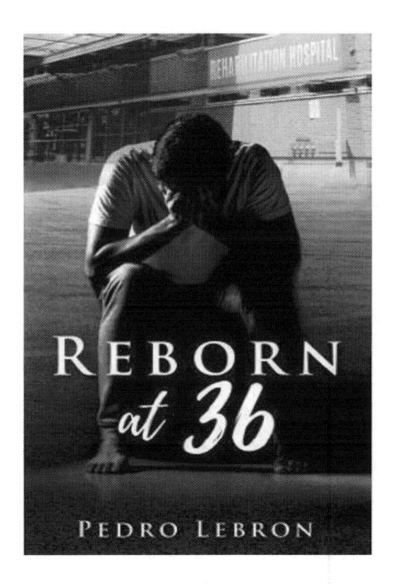

Reborn at 36

Reborn to life
Did God give me another chance because I saved my wife?,

I get happy I am here with kids, even with my dog
I can see the whole picture now, clear, I can see thru fog

I want to share a message, I need to share a story,
Only appreciating the simple, the little
things, can you reach true glory

I have been giving my family some headaches recuperating,
My persona is totally different, but I am working
hard, getting used to, demonstrating
That I am still a working man,
And I will keep working hard,
For my sisters, my friends, for my fam
It hasn't been easy, it's been hard,
I am still struggling, but I am still far

From being a good brother, a father, the husband I want to be
I need to be strong, I need to be focused,
Because I am facing reality

Life is what you make of it, better with no worries,
Life is what you make of it, life is truly, your story

www.rebornat36.com

What if you were forced to start your life all over? What would call it and what would you write?

_____

_____

_____

_____

_____

_____

_____

_____

_____

_____

_____

_____

_____

_____

_____

_____

REALITY

Reality

I wonder if sometimes I dwell too much on that moment
It drastically change my life, it has been nothing but a torment

I seemed to be blinded to what really is important in life
GOD SAID "hey dumb ass, you are letting
the beautiful things pass you by"

I have been through a very negative stage
Not easy to forget, not easy to turn the page

I have to be positive, I have to move forward
I have to get thru this negative stage, this horror

Set new goals, to shoot for them as I did in the past life
No more craziness no more wildlife
No more sins, no more unnecessary issues, no more strife
I have to behave, I need to change or no more wife

I love my family, my wife and my children
I have to provide, I have to be a father, I have
to be a man, that's a fact, nothing hidden

God kept me alive for a reason
You got to live your life to the fullest,
Enjoy every day, every season,
Definitely not a crime, no kind of treason

With all that said, I can't help wonder
What is next in life, I want a fun ride, a thunder
God show me the way, God please don't leave me under

Your Reality??

_____

_____

_____

_____

_____

_____

_____

_____

_____

_____

_____

_____

_____

_____

_____

_____

_____

_____

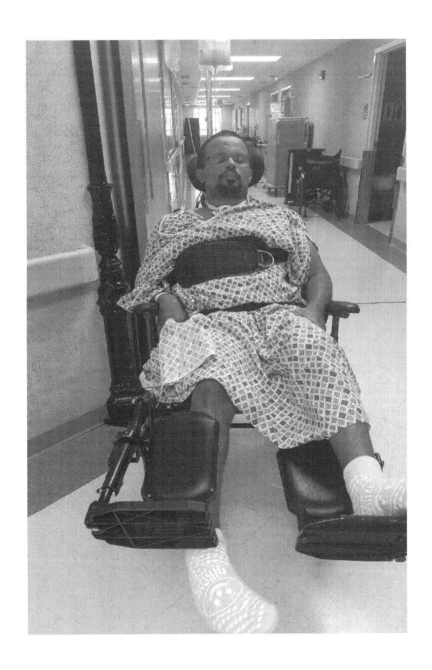

Recuperating From Coma

My brain was traumatically injured
I did not even know such a thing existed,
my whole self was triggered

I was dead when the ambulance picked
me up from the accident
I was given CPR, revived into a coma, and that was no incident

I only survived with 10% given that I would be
normal, 90% that I would be a vegetable,
Thank God that wasn't the case. Even the hospital
would call me miracle patient, acceptable

God works in mysterious ways
I know it was an answer to my own prayers,
Never expecting this, a little odd I say

When looking at me, you would say I lost everything
God gave a reset button, a second chance in life
and for that, I only want to sing

I got to a point in life where I put God aside
Not thinking straight, he figured, we
got to reset his hard drive

My hard drive was definitely reset
Now you can't put my faith to a test

I know he is there, I know he watches over us all the time
I love me some god, you got to figure, only
his way will everything be fine

I love life, I want to take advantage of the second opportunity
Live my life faithfully, Only with God
first....no other way, truthfully

Recuperating From ------??

_____

_____

_____

_____

_____

_____

_____

_____

_____

_____

_____

_____

_____

_____

_____

_____

_____

_____

PUERTO RICO

Puerto Rico

I lived in Puerto Rico from one to nine
I wasn't quite born there, my father was in the army
But Boricua to end, a Boricua full of pride

Living in Puerto Rico were the finest years of my life,
growing up playing with my cousins day in and day out
We are always together, playing baseball, being at the
beach, haciendo travesuras, that what it was all about

The last year I lived there, we had
hurricane Hugo, a category four
We moved to California, we had to move,
we were forced to take the tour

We left Puerto Rico after my mom's father
tragically died in our bathroom,
He died of a heart attack, a good man, an Army Soldier
We could no longer be near that bathroom,
it was now the darkroom

California was definitely a change for us all
We loved it, it was our new home
Getting there not speaking the language, everything
was strange, it definitely took a toll

I still get to visit Puerto Rico from time to time
It is our home, where we are from
Boricua Born, Boricua to the end, Boricua pride
Home

Fishing W/ Son

Going fishing with son
For every second I thank God a ton

We are trying to catch a good eating fish
Most likely we will get to go home with just catfish

Definitely not a qualified fisherman
But I thank God that I still can
Be alive and be with my fam

I give thanks every day that I am here
Not being able to spend time is what I fear

I have to concentrate and move forward
To live a positive and influential life
Definitely something to look towards

You cherish a moment with a loved one'

_____

_____

_____

_____

_____

_____

_____

_____

_____

_____

_____

_____

_____

_____

_____

_____

THE HARD WAY UP

The Hard Way Up

A life of crime
A life that use to be mine

I've done some things that are unspeakable
I have gotten away in ways that are unthinkable

From selling drugs and stealing cars
To being a baller but still far

From being a good working man
Responsible, caring, stable, but I am still far

From doing things that were only right
Had to learn to move forward and be focused
Far from it still, but not out of sight

To live a good life is something you learn,
Stay on the good side, do things the right,
and watch all the love you earn.

"THE HARD WAY UP" coming soon...

How did you grow up?

_____

_____

_____

_____

_____

_____

_____

_____

_____

_____

_____

_____

_____

_____

_____

_____

Mom

Raising three kids alone
you did it all on your own

we are all independent with our own businesses
you did a great job, we are all healthy with no illnesses

you put yourself thru school and went to work
you gave us a good comfortable life, we don't take it lightly,
we know it was not a joke

a woman to appreciate, a woman to admire
wow what a working woman, a woman not easily retired

you never gave up on us, you were always there,
no matter what we came across, you thought us to stand tall,
it was unbelievable, how much you cared

growing up i gave you some headaches
never forgetting those moments, i am sorry
i think about you all the time, and my soul aches

god took you a little early,
i can't express it enough, we love you and miss you.....dearly
we love you mom!

Someone very special to you.

_____

_____

_____

_____

_____

_____

_____

_____

_____

_____

_____

_____

_____

_____

_____

_____

_____

My Daughter Zeani

My love for you has no measure
I always think of you as my treasure

Thinking of what we went thru yesterday
makes me regret all my sins and all the
stupid things I did every day

I have never felt such concentrated pain
just imagining you not here, takes all of my energy
and how can I be obtained

From losing my mind, losing my focus and my whole self,
you are my sun, you are my light,
life without you makes no sense, and it's confusing all by itself
I pray for you to move forward, I pray for you to continue life
to be yourself, to make your own decisions
to not deal with everyday issues, to not deal with strife

Zeani I love you more than words can express,
to continue live without you, definitely makes no sense

I am very proud to call you my daughter,
and I will say it again.....I love you
and life without you really, really has no matter

Write to someone who looks up to you

Zeani Acielis

your first name is sea translated from Spanish
your middle name is sky translated the
same, clean with no tarnish

I love you more than words can express
and I know sometimes I put our relationship to a test

you make me want to be a better man, a more dedicated father
I love you dearly but I rather,

for us to get along, to have a better relationship
to be a father and daughter, the way is meant to be

your name has the same meaning in all language
beautiful, smart, strong, independent, the
full and complete awesome package

(Someone you adore????)

_____

_____

_____

_____

_____

_____

_____

_____

_____

_____

_____

_____

_____

_____

_____

_____

_____

_____

CONFUSED MAN

Confused Man

I live life happy
I am learning rapidly

I am not one to stress
I never get depress

But I feel I have so much inner pain
I even feel like crying,
sometimes I feel I cannot restrain

Feeling down and hopeless
Also feeling I can't do nothing
Feeling I am completely useless

Writing these poems seem to be therapeutic for me
It seems to help me relax, it seems to comfort me

I want to clear my mind, I want to be a good man,
I want to be a provider still, I want to be a man that still can

Stand tall and move my family forward,
Be a man to my family
Definitely something to look towards

A troubled or confused person?

_____

_____

_____

_____

_____

_____

_____

_____

_____

_____

_____

_____

_____

_____

_____

_____

MY PERSONALITY

My Personality

They talk about me
and they always judge me

I know I am not perfect
But I can care less what they expect

how they relate to me
how they distribute me
how they qualify me
And how they judge me

For any stupid thing
Without really knowing

What kind of person I am?
They judge me for anything bad, but really good I am

in between a hundred things well done
That I take advantage that I always have a tone

Without any advice, I always do my thing
with all the pride and concentration
in the middle of good and bad I feel myself between

I follow my path, without ever harming anyone.
A man with a bright future, a man that causes pain to no one

I follow my path, and with my own style
I continue my way, and only doing things right
God makes it all worthwhile

www.rebornat36.com

My Personality??

_____
_____
_____
_____
_____
_____
_____
_____
_____
_____
_____
_____
_____
_____
_____
_____
_____
_____

LIFE CHANGING EVENT

Life Changing Event

I have always been a working man
I am not design to be at home sitting like nothing can

From owning three companies for over ten years
To losing them with my accident so quick
with no time for even tears

How do you go from being the one and only provider?
To being the handicap man at home
And allowing your wife to now be the only income fighter

Always being the go to dude, the main
man, the center of attraction.
To now always feeling like I am a man falling
apart, a man with only fractions

I literally died and was not breathing
when the ambulance picked me up
I pray daily and I thank God a ton
But sometimes I get mad and I can't help feeling fired up

I have to learn and adapt myself to this new life
To live life one day at a time, take it slow
To only see this second chance as God's prize

www.rebornat36.com

35

You have had a very traumatic moment in your life. A Life Changing Event

_____

_____

_____

_____

_____

_____

_____

_____

_____

_____

_____

_____

_____

_____

_____

_____

_____

SISTERS

Letters to my Sisters

You have definitely played a role in this game
You two behaved like the true woman you are
True sisters, couldn't do it without you,
and you do nothing for fame

You two did what most persona could not stand
Like the true woman, I call sisters,.
what most people would say, like a man

You two took care of my family and my businesses
Only with your help, Love, and dedication
I was able to wake up to no problems and no illnesses

I feel with you on my team I could win any game
I can challenge anything and with the confidence you give me,
I will not to be allowed to be tamed

We bicker and fight,
I thank God I have 2 out of 3 women left, and with you
standing behind me,
I only feel like a man of height......lol

Letter to my ????

_____

_____

_____

_____

_____

_____

_____

_____

_____

_____

_____

_____

_____

_____

_____

_____

_____

MY DARLING

My Darling

OH, Darling my Darling
I love that song with your name

Unlike I said in the poem to my sisters,
that they do not do it for fame,
You deserve all the credit and all the love in this wifey game

I know it has not been easy putting up with me
You have learned to adapt yourself
To treat me like a third child, to literally babysit me

I love you more than words can express,
I know I sometimes put our relationship to a test
I would not change you, you are my best
Being able to call you my wife, I am truly blessed

Darling means to address a loved person
With you on my side
I only want to be a man, the true meaning in all versions

My ------

_____
_____
_____
_____
_____
_____
_____
_____
_____
_____
_____
_____
_____
_____
_____
_____
_____
_____

PERSONAL REFLECTION

Personal Reflection

I wrote a book about my life of crime
a pretty active teenage life I had
I thought I was untouchable, I walked
around acting like I was prime

I did things that are unspeakable
I got away in ways that are unthinkable

I should of went to jail for years
I thought I was going to be lock up,
losing my freedom I feared

I literally stole cars,
The dealership denied missing one
Therefore, the police could not put me behind bars

I consider all that to be a learning experience
Extremely lucky I am to be free
I am sorry you must read this.......Miriam

I am all grown up now, I would never.......
I have to be a responsible man; I have
to be focus on my new endeavor

"THE HARD WAY UP" book coming soon...

Personal Reflection??

_____

_____

_____

_____

_____

_____

_____

_____

_____

_____

_____

_____

_____

_____

_____

_____

_____

_____

_____

Mi Amigo Ruben

You were just a neighbor, but I liked you from the start
You had that old school feeling
You can tell you were easy going, a man with a good heart

From the Yauco Campos in Puerto Rico
Very cool, chill back, how they say in Spanish, magnifico

A good man to talk to, always understanding
Amigo means friend in Spanish
To have a drink with you always felt outstanding

I almost left this life with my accident
Apparently, it was in God's plan to take
you first without incident

It was devastating to see you go early,
A good friend, no matter the age difference, I miss you daily

I will still go visit your missis and your
children from time to time
I am going to miss you, may I get to someday
stand next to you and God, side to side.

REST IN PEACE RUBEN!

Mi Amigo ------

_____

_____

_____

_____

_____

_____

_____

_____

_____

_____

_____

_____

_____

_____

_____

_____

_____

_____

So Much Like Kyle

The son of a former client,
Running Jobs for him, you did good
You were always friendly, cool, very compliance

You suffered a Traumatic Brain Injury like me
Your injury was more complex
Unfortunately, it caused you more harm, more than it did me

It was sad to see a good dude go early
To see what happened to you,
you can't help but sometimes feel that
life doesn't treat you fairly

The experience with you was an eye-opener
you have tough me so much and I am sorry to see you go,
it seems like you here very, P, P, like the road-runner

I hope you rest in peace,
I pray for you and your dad both
May you find tranquility at heart, may
your pain really decrease.

REST IN PEACE KYLE!

So Much Like -----

_____

_____

_____

_____

_____

_____

_____

_____

_____

_____

_____

_____

_____

_____

_____

_____

_____

_____

_____

_____

_____

NEW PLANS

New Plans

In this life you must have plans
My life has drastically changed
I better get this out before shit hits the fan

It's hard to plan when it's hard to see the future
I don't know where I am, I don't know where I am standing,
I feel lost, I feel helpless, I feel like I have a brain tumor

I want to be a provider still
I want to take care of my family
Need to be a good man, I need to get over this problem hill

I am writing these books for now to see if
I can at least help with some income
To bring in a helping hand, to move my children forward
To look back at all of this, laugh, and
wonder how I was able to overcome

If you had new plans, what would they be?

_____

_____

_____

_____

_____

_____

_____

_____

_____

_____

_____

_____

_____

_____

_____

_____

_____

To Continue Life Without You

You have always been my Negra
We have been together so long, my love for you is
so strong, it veers off water like an umbrella

Negra means my dark skinned
I have always loved you so much, you are my prevailing wind

We have been together 22 years
Married after 20 years with each other
Not for nothing bad, I guess we wanted
to make sure we were peers

You cleaned my butt while in coma
I should be embarrassed, instead I am very proud of you
You prove me wrong, not something you
can expect from any persona

Our love for each other obviously has no measure
You are definitely worth more than any hidden treasure

We have created two beautiful extraordinary lives
To imagine life without you three, just
thinking about it give me hives

I LOVE YOU DARLING, ZEANI, & ISAIAH

To Continue Life ------- -----

_____

_____

_____

_____

_____

_____

_____

_____

_____

_____

_____

_____

_____

_____

_____

_____

_____

_____

_____

_____

The Lost of a True Icon

You were a man to follow, a man to listen
a true man at heart, a man that glisten

God took you early
for those of us that followed you,
we know you were definitely not treated fairly

"Only god can judge me know"

your ways were not easy to swallow
but everything you did made sense, your
words were true to life, yet somehow

We did not get to listen to all you had to say
I listen to your music, and I always pray
May god allow me to meet you someday
even in the afterlife, I will still be your
fan, I will listen to you all day

Your life was shortened on my birthday

thinking of you every year on that day
I chill with my boys and drink a bottle of Alize

We lost an icon when your life was taken
every time I think about it,
I feel pain, I can't help feeling shaken

A true thug from the start
I love that about you, I love that no matter what
you were always true to your heart

REST IN PEACE TUPAC!

Rest in Peace -----

REST IN PEACE 2PAC!
"THE ROSE THAT GREW FROM CONCRETE"
Tupac Shakur

Panama Steve

My brother from another mother
We met at 14 or 15, I don't remember
homies from the start, homies forever

We have done some shit, we have had fun, no doubt
A Boricua and Panamanian together,
some serious shit, watch out

We lost a loved one along the way
May you rest in peace Justin
May God allow us to see you again some day

We chill, we kick it, but don't get confused
If we have to get stupid
We will kick your ass Cali style, like them island fools

You are a good friend to me, a brother
Even my mom loved you like a son
May we be homies forever, chilling...with one another

Brother From Another Mother

_____

_____

_____

_____

_____

_____

_____

_____

_____

_____

_____

_____

_____

_____

_____

_____

_____

_____

_____

_____

_____

A BRIGHT FUTURE

A Bright Future

I have been thru a negative stage
It has not been easy turning the page

It is time to look ahead, time to look forward
I must move on, I must look towards

A bright and uplifting future, eventually
Got to look ahead and focus on financial stability, actually

I have written and published a couple of books,
Hoping that will help my financials and get me off the hook

I am not used to being the handicap Dad at home
But this is life for me now, I have to get it to my dome

I will concur this topic, this stage
I am not one to give up, I am definitely not one to cave

A Bright Future

_____

_____

_____

_____

_____

_____

_____

_____

_____

_____

_____

_____

_____

_____

_____

_____

_____

_____

My Homie Justin

God took you early my friend
We didn't get to say goodbye, but we will be friends to the end

We use to hang out, kicked it, playing
ball in the middle of the night
You were a cool dude, chilling with you
and the boys always felt right

You played basketball funny as hell, but you were good,
You kicked our ass playing, we laughed, all good in the hood

You were always easy going and down for whatever,
We miss you, we love you, we will be boys forever

May we have a drink, look back at old times and laugh
Friends forever, I hope to see you again,
I want to see you in person, not just a photograph

My Homie ------

Shirley

I love you homie, you have always been a good friend
May we always chill, kick back, be homies forever....to the end

Please excuse me with my friend Hassan
I have always looked to you as a homie, nothing more,
Hassan, you are so much cooler than that idiot Shawn...lol

Shirley, you and I have always hung out, done whatever
I love to be your friend, I loved to go out with you
May we dance forever

I was so sorry when you lost your mother
I have been there too, I lost mine, I know the feeling
that's why we were there to comfort each other

I can't believe your **** move to Cali
To much of a coincidence, they just made it legal there,
The ganja, the Buddha, the MARI-juana

I hope to chill with you someday in my old hood,
Drive you thru my old streets, my old hangouts
Lay back, reminisce on old times, smoke
a big fat one too....all good

My Best Friend

_____

_____

_____

_____

_____

_____

_____

_____

_____

_____

_____

_____

_____

_____

_____

_____

_____

_____

_____

_____

WRITE HERE
WRITE NOW

Write Here Write Now

I am writing now
My life is a mess, how did I get to this
point and so quick?, WOW

I have always been a man that has accomplished many things
I feel so lost now, After my accident, I feel I can't do a thing

Don't get me wrong, I really appreciate been here
God gave me another chance,
with him in my life I can be certain, I can live with no fear

Accomplishments seem so much harder now
I have to stay focused, got to move forward, yet somehow

I have to be a go getter, have to be a positive role model.
I have to continue to fight, I have to live
a positive life, with no scandal

Show my kids how to stand tall
To move forward, to always strive for more, to never stall

I must concentrate and focus on my new project
Don't quite know what that is yet, but
I will once again earn their respect, do more than they expect
To be a man, to continue to fight for more
I want to be a good example for my kids, I will win this war

I pray to God to show me the way, to
point me in the right direction,
With him as my guide, I will do what's right,
Earn their love again, their affection

I have adapted, I have learned to live one day at a time
I must strive and accomplish more, I will continue to climb

For now, I will continue to write and
express my feelings this way
Maybe writing my intentions and motivation on paper
will cure my mind and clear my airways

Write Here, Write Now

THE THREE WOMAN IN MY LIFE

The Three Woman in my Life

I have three women in my life,
My two sisters and Darling which I now call my wife

They have never gotten along,
But they are the most important woman in
my life, my love for them is so strong

They cannot get along with one another
They bicker, they fight
But when they had no choice over me,
they had to work with each other

After my accident, the doctors were talking
about me as if I was going to be a vegetable
It must have been hard, mind-boggling
But they manage to stay strong, work
with each other, acceptable

I would not be here if it were not for them
I was able to wake up, be myself, make my own decisions,
Thank God of course, but I owe my recovery to three of them

My sisters and I now do not have the
same relationship anymore,
We have always been very close, but
now we are not getting along
It does not feel right with the sisters who I absolutely adore

This injury is by far the weirdest injury you can endure
Leave it up to me, if you would know me, you would
know that I would be one to get it, and be cured

My best friend stated when I was in a coma,
That if ever there was anyone, That I would be the one to get
it, brag about it, stating I survived it, like I deserved a diploma

Now I got it, I survived it, and I want to move on
My sisters and my wife, I want us all to get along
I want us to be a team, to work together, to not be drawn

The ----- ------ in my Life

Where am I Headed?

I must stay focus
I must look forward, be positive and not be so loco

I can help wonder where my live is headed
Always had so much, always worked hard, always had big goals
I always knew what to do, where I was going, forget it

Have you ever stopped to think what is best
Unfortunately, I have no answer, I don't know what's next

Me entire family is pushing me to get disability
I am not design to be the handicap man at home
Do nothing, wait for a small check once a month, no way...
there is no possibility

I will figure something out,
I will be a man to my family, and be all about

Taking care of them, earning a living, provide stability
Be a man to my wife, a father to my kids, perform
to my full potential, use all of my abilities

Where am I Headed?

_____

_____

_____

_____

_____

_____

_____

_____

_____

_____

_____

_____

_____

_____

_____

_____

_____

_____

_____

NEXT

Next

I do not know where I am going
I got drama popping up left and right, it seems to be on-going

Now, it is really difficult see what kind of man I am going to be
I need to be strong, I need to hold on, no
matter what the outcome, you will see

It's hard to know where this life is taking me
I will go for the ride, enjoy it, never thinking
of the damage it can due to me

Like in that movie, Forrest Gump ....
"Life is like a box of chocolate,
U will never know what u are going to get"
I am alive, I will take the ride, God's gift, I will
never forget

There is no book, no instructions that can tell me what to do
I have to figure it out, I have to be positive,
not worry about what the outcome will do

I do not know what is next in my life
With God on my side, I must enjoy the
ride, I will follow his ways,
Live the best life that I can, till my afterlife

Next

FOGGY PATH

Foggy Path

You ever feel so lost
You start to have bad uncontrollable thoughts?

Damaging all the things you believed in
You know they are so wrong
You are so lost, you will not achieve them

What can you do?, your path back home seems so foggy
I can't see clearly, but I will find my way back, chilling,
thinking about it while smoking a cigar, a stogy

I pray that God shows me the way, may he clear my path
Guide me in the right direction, don't let me get distracted
by an intersection, learn to control my wrath

I have never felt so confused
So unsure of my to dos
Completely ignorant of what to do
next, to be that man I refuse

I pray that I find my way
I will secure my destiny, rest assure, I will take advantage
of this second opportunity, and that is all I have to say

Foggy Path

_____

_____

_____

_____

_____

_____

_____

_____

_____

_____

_____

_____

_____

_____

_____

_____

_____

_____

My Champion

The person I call my wife is my champ
She is the only person I need in my corner,
the only fighter I need in my camp

She has been dealing with my recuperation, which is not easy
While at the same time taking care of our
beautiful daughter's condition
She is amazing, how she deals with it?
the situation is very uneasy

I grow to love her more and more every day
I have been a fool in the past, not
appreciating the woman I have
I have loved you always, way more now since we left the Bay

I lie if I say I can't love you more
I have noticed my love for you grows each day
You are absolutely someone who I can only adore

Lately, I have really noticed how important
it is to have you in my life,
I am sorry for all the drama, all the drastic
changes we have been thru lately
I want to hold on to you, I want to love
spoil you even in the afterlife

My Champion

_____
_____
_____
_____
_____
_____
_____
_____
_____
_____
_____
_____
_____
_____
_____
_____
_____

ARTHUR

An Arthur Now

I never thought that this is what I would be doing
I have written four books
Life is unpredictable, you never know where you are going

Trust me, I have never been a book reader
To be one of those guys that hangs out at the libraries
I have always looked at those guys as strange breeders

I have written four books in less than a years' time,
Including all the poems in this book, out my sisters and I
I am the last one you thought would be doing this, but ok fine

If you knew me, you would think what
happen to me was treason
Actually, what happened to me was for all the good reasons

For that, I thought my story needed to be shared
Believe me, I have a very positive story, at first, I thought,
how do I dare?
I actually love to share, that is why I tell it with a flare
Never thought I would be doing this, I
thought people wouldn't care

People need to do the same, believe, do not lose your faith,
my life was darkness, God has given a
light, I needed him to interface

An ------ Now

40 NOW

40 Now

I cannot believe I am 40 now
I almost did not make it this far
I feel so lucky and so blessed…. WOW

I am so happy I get to be with my beautiful
wife & see my kids grow up
To whom besides God can I say thank
you to, there is no runner up

Life is a little confusing, I do not know
what to do with this second chance
Definitely going to be a good man, appreciate being here
To live another life with different views, there is no advance

When you are a young buck you never
picture getting to this age,
You never know what you will be doing
An unpredictable time in your life, a
new project I need to engage

I just need to turn 40 and turn the page,
I never thought I would be here, I never
thought I would get to this stage

Rather, I just need to be happy and visit the cantina
Time to party, enjoy your loved ones, time for tequila

Your Age

9/11

I want to celebrate I finished my book, but I cannot
forget This is a sad day, we lost so many on this
hurtful day, this day was a complete threat

All I want to do is pray
So many lives, tons of people, freights,
so many people feeling gray

When I got to work, so many people were sad
I was out of it, I didn't know what was going on
So many people were now absent, so many people hurt bad

I would have a hard time each and every year
My birthday is on the 13th, I cannot celebrate
without being afraid or having tears

May God give peace of mind to all those families
I can't imagine what they have been thru....the pain, the agony

REST IN PEACE 9/11

9/11

_____

_____

_____

_____

_____

_____

_____

_____

_____

_____

_____

_____

_____

_____

_____

_____

_____

_____

FEELINGS, CONFUSED

Feelings, Confused

I know where I am at but I still feel lost
My mind is a mess but I still think
clearly enough to understand
Everything seems so confusing but I still
know what needs to be done first
I fight with my sisters but I still need them in my life
I crave for my wife's attention but I don't seek it
My mind is a complete mess but I don't search for clarity
I am hoping with time it becomes clear even
after the mess I feel we are in
I feel lost with little fear that I will find my way
Hopeless but hard to find hope
Careless but being very caring
Not worry much but completely stressed
Hard to see it but I still see
Stressed to be me but me I am
Confusing to see where I am going but I am still going
Right now life is not to clear but I will see it thru

Feelings, Confused

TRAUMATIC BRAIN INJURY

Traumatic Brain Injury

Traumatic brain injury is what I suffered
I never thought your brain can be even injured, awkward

Doctors stated 90% that I would be a vegetable
Thank God, they were wrong this time, acceptable

I was forced to restart my life
A second chance, a new life, I have to be sharp like a knife

Easier said than done
Adapt to old ways and learn all new ones, really, no fun

It makes you appreciate the little things
To waste no time, enjoy every moment & see
what this second life has to bring

I wonder why I received another chance
When so many others don't, why do I get to advance?

I hope one day to know, but right now
all I can do is thank God a tone
I am so grateful for this second opportunity, because
of him I get to be here in flesh and bone

Whatever he wants from me, I hope to do it right
That's really important to me, to get it right, I will fight

My Injury

_____

_____

_____

_____

_____

_____

_____

_____

_____

_____

_____

_____

_____

_____

_____

_____

_____

_____

_____

_____

Dad....Yuyo

Dad....or how your family use to call you, YUYO
You weren't a good father, a dependable
guide, my mom had to find a new home

It wasn't your fault, you had a confused life
You had a difficult youth, a wildlife

You didn't act the same after your
brother was tragically killed,
His death was very damaging to you, his spot you never filled

Something you did and he paid the ultimate price
You were never the same, you two had rollen the diced

I thank God that I included myself in
the last few years of your life
At least, I got to know what it was like to have a
father, enjoy all of you until your afterlife

I liked you, I miss you, I love you
I am still your son, I would not have it any other way,
I don't care what anybody says about you

Dad

_____

_____

_____

_____

_____

_____

_____

_____

_____

_____

_____

_____

_____

_____

_____

_____

_____

_____

Al el lado de cada poema yo a dejado un espacio para que usted escriba su propio poema usando un titulo igual que el mio o paredico. El ganador va hacer publicado en mi proximo libro. Puede enviar su poema a la dirección de email alistado a el final de este libro.

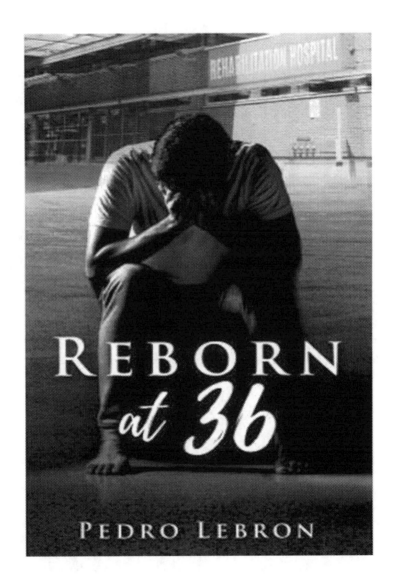

REBORN
at 36

PEDRO LEBRON

Renacio a Los 36

Renacío a la vida
¿Dios me dio otra oportunidad porque salvé a
mi esposa y no permití la alternativa?

Me alegro de estar aquí con mis hijos, incluso con mi perra,
Puedo ver todo el panorama ahora, claro,
puedo ver a mi familia aquí en la tierra

Quiero compartir un mensaje, necesito compartir una historia,
Sólo apreciando lo simple, las pequeñas cosas,
se puede llegar a verdadera gloria

He estado dando a mi familia algunos
dolores de cabeza recuperándome
Mi personaje es totalmente diferente,
pero estoy acostumbrándome, demostrándole
Que sigo siendo un hombre trabajador,

Y seguiré luchando duro,
Para mis hermanas, mis amigos, mi familia
No ha sido fácil, pero de eso estoy seguro

Todavía estoy luchando, pero todavía estoy lejos
De ser un buen hermano, un padre, un
esposo y no tan aventurero

Necesito ser fuerte, necesito estar en paz
Porque me enfrento a una diferente realidad

La vida es lo que haces de ella, mejor sin preocupaciones,
La vida es lo que haces de ella, la vida
es realmente, tu dedicación

www.renacioalos36.com

Renacio a Los --

MI PERSONA

Mi Persona

Hablan de mi
Pero que me importa

No soy Perfecto
Pero siempre bien alerto

A lo que relacionan conmigo
Y como me distribuyen
Y como me quilifican
Y como me judgan

Por cualquier estupidez
Sin de verdad saber

Que clase persona yo soy
Me judgan por un Mal, pero aquí estoy

Entre cien bienes echo
Que yo soy una persona de aprovecho

Sin ningún consejo
Tus ases lo tuyo
Pero con todo El orgullo

Tu sigues tu Camino
Sin hacerle daño a nadie.
Un hombre con futuro

Y con tu propio estilo
Continuas tu camino
Y Dios sigue contigo

Mi Persona

_____

_____

_____

_____

_____

_____

_____

_____

_____

_____

_____

_____

_____

_____

_____

_____

_____

_____

_____

MI DARLING

Mi Darling

Hay Darling mi Darling
La canción dice tu nombre

No como les escribí a mis hermanas que no lo hacen por fama
Te mereces todo el crédito, no le pones atención a el drama

Yo sé que no ha sido fácil aguantarme
Yo sé que has tenido a que adatarte
Yo soy tu tercer hijo ahora y tienes que acostumbrarte

Yo te amo más que las palabras se pueden expresar,
Se que a veces pongo nuestra relación a probar

Yo no te cambiaria, tú eres mi premio
Contento de llamarte mis esposa, cualquier
otra mujer, te queda a medio

TE AMO DARLING!

Mi ------

EL CAMINO DIFICIL HACIA ARRIBA

El Camino Difícil Hacia Arriba

Una vida de crimen
Una vida que era firme
A echo algunas cosas inesperadas
Me a escapado en maneras que nunca te las imaginaras

De vender drogas y robarme autos
Ha ser un tipo de calle y sin faltos

De ser un buen trabajador
cariñoso, fuerte, responsable y un buen ejecutor

De hacer las cosas correctas
E pasado diferentes etapas, una trifecta

Moverme adelante y quedarme enfocado
Lejos todavía, pero no me a equivocado

De vivir una vida correcta es algo bueno de aprender
Quedarte en el lado bueno, hacer las cosas
bien y veras que serias fácil de querer

"EL CAMINO DIFICIL HACIA ARRIBA" Libro viene pronto!

El Camino Difícil Hacia Arriba

My Friend Ruben

Sólo eras un vecino, pero me gustabas desde el principio.
Tuviste esa sensación de la vieja escuela, un buen inicio

Se puede decir que era fácil comunicarse con usted,
un hombre con buen corazón, un hombre de buena fe

Desde los Campos Yauco en Puerto Rico
Un hombre que le gustaba la siembra, magnifico

Un hombre que era bueno, siempre relajado
Friend quiere decir amigo en ingles
Tomar una copa con usted siempre se sintió extraordinario

Casi morí cuando tuve mi accidente
Aparentemente,
El plan de Dios era llevarlo a usted
primero y desafortunadamente,

Fue devastarte verlo irse temprano,
Un buen amigo, no importa la diferencia de edad,
siempre lo considere un buen hermano,

Todavía iré a visitar a su señora y a sus hijos de vez en cuando
Continuar la vida sin usted va a hacer difícil, pero,
hay que seguir caminando y caminando

Siempre lo voy a extrañar, que algún día
Dios me deje verlo otra vez
Que volvamos hacer vecinos, el la próxima vida, tal vez

QUE DESCANSES EN PAZ RUBEN!

My Friend -----

_____

_____

_____

_____

_____

_____

_____

_____

_____

_____

_____

_____

_____

_____

_____

_____

_____

_____

_____

Continuar la Vida Sin Ti

Siempre has sido mi Negra
Hemos estado juntos tanto tiempo, mi
amor por ti es tan fuerte
que le cogí cariño hasta la suegra

Dark Skinned significa negra
Siempre te he amado tanto, estar al lado tuyo, me alegra

Hemos estado juntos 22 años
Casados después de 20 años juntos
No por nada malo, solo quería asegurarme y punto

Me limpiaste el trasero mientras estabas en coma
Debería estar avergonzado, Demuestras que me equivoco,
no es algo que puedas esperar de cualquier persona

Nuestro amor uno por el otro obviamente no puede ser medido
Definitivamente vales más que un tesoro escondido

Hemos creado dos hermosas vidas extraordinarias
Imaginar la vida sin ustedes tres, es continuar
la vida como una rompida maquinaria

¡LOS AMO A LOS TRES!

Continuar la Vida Sin Ti

Abuela

Usted me a ensenado como amar incondicional
una mujer mayor, una mujer bella, tradicional

Estar junto a el lado tuyo es una bendición
yo la quiero señora, usted es mi vieja,
una mujer llena de tradición

No me puedo imaginar la vida sin usted
una mujer buena, extraordinaria
completamente llena de buena fe

Mi Abuelo y mi Pascuala
ustedes siempre han sido importante para mi
no Pascuala es Panchi, perdona, no se me ponga enojada

Panchi es un nombre que jamás se me olvidara
usted es la mujer más importante en mi vida
usted siempre a sido tan buena, yo sé que
Dios siempre me la acompañara

LA AMO MI VIEJA!

Grandma

_____

_____

_____

_____

_____

_____

_____

_____

_____

_____

_____

_____

_____

_____

_____

_____

_____

_____

_____

Suegra

Nunca pensé que le iba coger cariño a la SUEGRA
Cuando empecé con su hija, me tenía bien
advertido, me tenía a pruebas

Yo la considero un amor, una segunda Madre
Una mujer completa, una mujer que se puede
comportar como Los dos, Madre y Padre

Yo le tengo mucho respeto, mucho cariño
me gusta pasar tiempo con usted,
No se me olvida que tengo que portarme
bien, o si no me fastidio

Una SUEGRA con quien se puede pasar buen rato, joder, balla
Reírse un rato, fumarse un NICA PADRON y darse
un palito de FLOR DE CANA......NICOYA!

Sin usted yo y Darling no fueranos familia
Que Díos nos la deje aquí por ochenta años mas
Yo le prometo cuidar su hija y sus nietos, una promesa sencilla.

LA ADORO MI SUEGRA!

Mother in Law

REFLEXIÓN PERSONAL

Reflexión Personal

Escribí un libro sobre mi vida en crimen
una vida de adolescente bien activa, una vida firme

Pensaba que era intocable,
caminé por ahí actuando como
no podía ser tocado, impresionable

Hice cosas que son indescriptibles
Me escapé en maneras que jamás te la imaginaras, increíble

Debí de ir a la cárcel por años
pensé que iba a estar encerrado,
perdiendo mi libertad, gracias a Dios, fue un desengaño

Hasta me robaba nuevos autos
El concesionario negó perder un auto
la policía no pudo poderme tras las rejas,
bien frustrados, que falto

Considero todo esto ser una experiencia de aprendizaje
extremamente suerte tengo de estar libre
por favor, Miriam mi suegra, no lea este mensaje,

He crecido ahora, estoy mucho más maduro
tengo que ser un hombre responsable,
tengo que estar enfocado en mi nuevo futuro

Reflexión Personal

_____

_____

_____

_____

_____

_____

_____

_____

_____

_____

_____

_____

_____

_____

_____

_____

HOMBRE CONFUNDIDO

Hombre Confundido

Vivo la vida felizmente
Estoy aprendiendo rápidamente

No soy de los que se estresa
Nunca me deprimo, una promesa

Pero siento que tengo tanto dolor interno
Incluso a veces tengo ganas de llorar,
a veces me siento como que estoy en el infierno

Sentirme confundido y desesperado
También sentir que no puedo hacer nada
Sentir que soy completamente inútil, frustrado

Escribir estos poemas parece ser terapéutico para mí
Parece que me ayuda a relajarme, parece consolarme a mi

Quiero despejar mi mente, quiero ser un buen hombre,
Quiero ser un proveedor todavía, quiero ser
un hombre para mi familia, costumbre

Mantenerme un hombre alto y mover
a mi familia hacia adelante,
Definitivamente algo para mirar en el futuro
y definitivamente no frustrarme

Hombre Confundido

_____

_____

_____

_____

_____

_____

_____

_____

_____

_____

_____

_____

_____

_____

_____

_____

_____

_____

UN FUTURO BRILLANTE

Un Futuro Brillante

He pasado por una etapa negativa
No ha sido fácil cambiar a una etapa menos activa

Es el momento de mirar hacia adelante, para el frente
tengo que mirar hacia un futuro positivo, futuro brillante

Tengo que concentrarme y estabilizar mis financieras
He escrito y publicado un par de libros
Esperando que me ayude un poco, como quiera

No estoy acostumbrado a ser el papá deshabilitado en casa
Pero, esta es la vida para mí ahora,
tengo que acostumbrarme, no importa lo que pasa

Conquistare este tema, esta etapa
No soy una persona que se rinde,
Soy una persona que sigue en la lucha, peliando y no se escapa

Un Futuro Brillante

_____

_____

_____

_____

_____

_____

_____

_____

_____

_____

_____

_____

_____

_____

_____

_____

_____

CARTA A MIS HERMANA

Carta a Mis Hermanas

Definitivamente han jugado un papel en este juego
Ustedes dos se comportaron como la
verdadera mujeres que son
Mujeres increíbles, Mujeres a Fuego

Ustedes dos hicieron lo que la mayoría de
la persona no pudieran soportar
Como las dos verdaderas mujeres, yo llamo hermanas.
Como ustedes nadie se puede comportar

Ustedes dos cuidaron de mi familia y mis negocios
Sólo con tu ayuda, amor y dedicación
Pude despertarme sin problemas y sin
enfermedades, mi testimonio

Siento que yo con ustedes podría ganar cualquier partido
Puedo desafiar cualquier cosa y con la confianza que me dan,
Puedo conquistar lo que sea, y con ustedes
en mi equipo, nunca a perdido

Hablamos y Peleamos,

Pero le doy gracias a Dios me quedan 2 de 3 mujeres,
Con las dos paradas de tras de mi
Puedo conquistar cualquier tema y siempre ganar los deberes

¡MIS HEROES!

Carta a Mis ------

_____

_____

_____

_____

_____

_____

_____

_____

_____

_____

_____

_____

_____

_____

_____

_____

_____

GALDO

Galdo

Galdo,
No te pude Ir a verte a lo último perdona, que falto

La última vez que te vi, hacen anos
Estavanos pasándola bien, dándonos un trago, sin daño

Tú eras uno de los más jóvenes tíos
Siempre fuiste chévere conmigo, no poder visitarte
esta cabron, hasta me da calofrió

Dios te llevo muy temprano,
tu siempre fuiste bien cool, ya no estás aquí, acho mano

Puerto Rico no es igual visitar sin ti
Que Dios te Bendiga y te tenga en la gloria hasta el fin

Que descanses en paz brother
Aquí sentada al lado mío mientras yo escribo esta your mother

Abuela se pone triste cuando pregunto sobre ti
Te extraño, te amo tío
Estoy pensando en ti

Family

_____

_____

_____

_____

_____

_____

_____

_____

_____

_____

_____

_____

_____

_____

_____

_____

_____

_____

LA REALIDAD

La Realidad

Mi vida cambió drásticamente
no ha sido más que un tormento, específicamente

Parece que estoy cegado a lo que realmente
es importante en la vida
DIOS DIJO "oye pendejo, estás dejando
pasar las cosas importantes,
Esto solo fue una pequeña caída

He pasado por una etapa muy negativa
No es fácil olvidar esta página, hay que pensar en la alternativa

Tengo que ser positivo, tengo que seguir adelante
Tengo que conquistar esta etapa negativa,
concentrarme en lo importante

Establecer nuevos objetivos como lo hice en la vida pasada
No más locura, No más pecados, no más problemas,
Tengo que comportarme, o continuar
como que tengo la vida apagada

Amo a mi familia, a mi esposa y a mis hijos
Tengo que proveer, tengo que ser un padre,
tengo que ser un hombre fijo

Dios me mantuvo vivo por una razón
Disfrutar todos los días, cada temporada,
vivir la vida y no ser tan cabezón

¿Con todo lo dicho, no puedo evitar
preguntarme lo que sigue en la vida?
quiero gozar un paseo divertido, Dios deme un trueno,
Dios por favor déjeme gozar la vida antes de mi partida

La Realidad

_____

_____

_____

_____

_____

_____

_____

_____

_____

_____

_____

_____

_____

_____

_____

_____

_____

_____

Mami

La vida no es igual sin ti
Yo escribí un poema sobre ti,

Se llama Mom
¡Hablamos de la cosa increíble que tu
cumpliste, te extraño un montón!

No hay ningún poema que pueda describir
lo increíble que tu fuiste
Tu fuiste una madre impresionante, no hay ninguna
cosa que nos faltaba, tú siempre nos cumplistes

Una madre como tú jamás se puede remplazar
Yo nunca ha pasado un tiempo más difícil
que cuando te enfermaste
Nunca pensé que te fueras a enfermar

Contigo me di de cuenta que extremo es el cáncer
Una enfermedad terrible, te quita a los que amas,
absolutamente nada que se pueda hacer,
todavía no hay ningún avance

Tu siempre fuiste una mujer, una madre intocable
Siempre nos cuidabas, nos atendías,
nos guiabas, bien responsable

Te amo madre una cantidad inesperada
yo te quiero volver a ver, besarte, abrasarte,
Que dios me permita otra vez, compartir un tiempo contigo,
y hablarte

¡TE AMO MAI!

Mami

_____

_____

_____

_____

_____

_____

_____

_____

_____

_____

_____

_____

_____

_____

_____

_____

_____

_____

_____

FRUSTRADO Y ESTRESADO

Frustrado y Estresado

Últimamente siempre me siento frustrado
La mente mía es un reguero, confundido y estresado

Yo siempre fui una persona positiva
una persona trabajadora, bien activa

Ahora no puedo trabajar y no puedo hacer na
me siento inútil, como que no puedo contemplar

Esta vida ahora no la entiendo
nada es igual, como que todo es diferente, no la comprendo

¿Qué me toca hacer ahora?
yo quiero tener una vida interesante, una vida que explora

Explorar lo extraño, lo que es diferente
pero quiero hacerlo con mi familia, yo amo a mi gente

quiero movernos para el frente, hacia adelante
ensenarles a mis hijos los valores, las cosas importantes

Le doy gracias a Dios por la segunda oportunidad
aunque mi vida es completamente diferente
tengo que enfrentarme a esta nueva realidad

Frustrado y Estresado

_____

_____

_____

_____

_____

_____

_____

_____

_____

_____

_____

_____

_____

_____

_____

_____

Panama Steve

Mi hermano de otra madre
Nos conocimos a los 14 o 15 años, no recuerdo
Amigos desde el principio, Amigos para siempre

Hemos hecho un desmadre, pero nos hemos divertido,
sin duda
Un Boricua y Panameño juntos, algo bien serio, pide ayuda

Perdimos a unos de los seres queridos
Que descanses en paz Justin
Que Dios nos permita verte de nuevo,
tu inesperada partida, la emos sentido

Relajamos y jodemos, pero no te confundas
Si tenemos que ponernos bravo
Te romperemos la madre, como dicen
los mexicanos, sin preguntas

Eres un buen amigo para mí, un hermano
Incluso mi mamá te amaba como un hijo
Que seamos amigos para siempre, mi hermano urbano

Hermano de Otra Madre

PROXINO

Próximo

No sé adónde voy
Tengo drama apareciendo de derecha a izquierda,
no es la clase de persona que soy

Ahora, es muy difícil ver qué nuevo hombre voy a ser
Necesito ser fuerte, necesito enfrentarme no
importa cuál sea el resultado, veremos a ver

Es difícil saber adónde me lleva esta vida
Tomare el paseo, lo disfrutaré, sin pensar en mi seria herida

Como dicen en la película con Forrest Gump....
"La vida es como una caja de chocolate,
nunca sabrás lo que va a ofrecer"
Estoy vivo todavía, voy a tomar el paseo, un
regalo de Dios, y la voy a sostener

No hay libro, no hay instrucciones que
puedan decirme qué hacer hoy en día
Tengo que averiguarlo, tengo que ser positivo,
no preocuparme por el resultado todavía

No sé qué sigue próximo en esta vida
Con Dios a mi lado, debo disfrutar el viaje, seguiré su
camino, vivir la mejor vida, aunque no sea conocida

Próximo

_____

_____

_____

_____

_____

_____

_____

_____

_____

_____

_____

_____

_____

_____

_____

_____

_____

40 ANOS AHORA

40 Anos Ahora

No puedo creer que tengo 40 años ahora, increíble
Casi no llego tan lejos
Me siento tan afortunado y bendecido de estar aquí, sensible

Estoy tan feliz de poder estar con mi bella
esposa y ver a mis hijos crecer
A quien además de Dios puedo darle
las gracias, no hay finalista,
solo él lo puede hacer

La vida es un poco confusa, no sé qué hacer
con esta segunda oportunidad
Definitivamente voy a ser un buen hombre, ver todo positivo
Vivir otra vida con diferentes puntos de vista, no es felicidad

Cuando eres un joven nunca te imaginas llegar a esta edad,
No sabes lo que vas a hacer,
un momento impredecible en tu vida, un
nuevo proyecto tengo que obtener

Sólo necesito cumplir 40 años y pasar la página,
Nunca pensé que estaría aquí, nunca
pensé que llegaría a esta etapa,
Estar aquí es una bendición de Dios, mi vida se siente mágica

Más bien, sólo necesito ser feliz y visitar la cantina
Hora de salir a fiestar, disfrutar a los seres querido,
hora para el tequila

Tu Edad

_____

_____

_____

_____

_____

_____

_____

_____

_____

_____

_____

_____

_____

_____

_____

_____

_____

_____

CONFUNDIDOS, SENTIMIENTOS

Confundidos, Sentimientos

Sé dónde estoy, pero todavía me siento perdido
Mi mente es un desastre, pero todavía pienso
lo suficientemente claro para entender
Todo parece tan confuso, pero todavía
sé lo que hay que hacer primero
Lucho con mis hermanas, pero todavía las necesito en mi vida
Anhelo la atención de mi esposa, pero no la busco.
Mi mente es un completo desastre, pero no busco claridad
Espero con el tiempo se hace claramente evidente incluso
después del lío que siento que estamos metidos
Me siento perdido con poco miedo de
que voy a encontrar mi camino
Desesperanza, pero difícil de encontrar esperanza
Descuidado, pero siendo muy cariñoso
No me preocupo mucho pero completamente estresado
Difícil de ver, pero todavía veo
Estresado de ser yo, pero yo soy
Confusa para ver a dónde voy, pero sigo yendo
En este momento la vida no está clara, pero
puedo voy a ver a través de ella

Confundidos, Sentimientos

Mi Campeon

La persona a la que llamo mi esposa es mi campeón
Ella es la única persona que necesito en mi esquina, y
perdóname, en esa foto te queda bien ese mahón

Ella a estado lidiando con mi recuperación, lo cual no es fácil
Mientras que al mismo tiempo cuidar a nuestra hermosa
hija y con su condición, Ella es increíble, ella es mami

Yo a sido un tonto en el pasado, no
apreciando a la mujer que tengo
Te he amado siempre, tu eres la mujer más
importante en mi vida, pendejo si no te sostengo

Miento si digo que no puedo amarte más,
me a dado de cuenta que mi amor por
ti crece cada día mas y mas
Tenerte en mi vida, verte todos los días,
estar junto a ti, eso es mi melodía

Últimamente, he notado lo importante
que es tenerte en mi vida,
Lo siento por todo el drama, todos los cambios
drásticos que hemos pasado en estos ultimo días

Mi Campeon

_____

_____

_____

_____

_____

_____

_____

_____

_____

_____

_____

_____

_____

_____

_____

_____

_____

_____

PUERTO RICO

Puerto Rico

Viví en Puerto Rico de uno a nueve años
No nací allí, mi padre estaba en el ejército
No importa, un boricua puro, un Boricua lleno de orgullo, coño

Living in Puerto Rico fueron los mejores años de mi vida,
Criándome y jugando con mis primos día tras día
Siempre estamos juntos, jugando béisbol, haciendo travesuras,
como si fuera una fantasía

estuvimos en el huracán Hugo, una categoría cuatro
Nos mudamos a California, tuvimos que mudarnos,
nos vimos obligados, todo confuso, nada claro

Nos fuimos de Puerto Rico después que el padre de
mi madre murió trágicamente en nuestro baño,
Murió de un ataque al corazón, un buen soldado
La partida de el nos hiso mucho daño

California fue definitivamente un cambio para todos,
era nuestro nuevo hogar, no sabíamos hablar el idioma,
pero, de todos modos

todavía voy a visitar Puerto Rico de vez en cuando
nuestra casa, de donde somos
boricua nacido, Boricua hasta el final, Boricua cantando

Home

Papi.....Yuyo

Papi....cómo te desia la familia.....YUYO!
no fuietes un buen guía, un padre con orgullo

Yo sé que tuviste una vida confusa
no fue tu culpa. te criaste de una manera intrusa

No quedastes igual después que mataron a tu hermano
la muerte de él te hiso mucho daño, tú y el eran bien cercano

Algo hicieron y él tuvo que pagar el precio
nunca fuites el mismo. tu mirabas la via con un desprecio

Yo le doy gracias a dios que me incluí
en tus últimos años de tu vida
por los menos pude disfrutarte y sertime como
que tuve un padre, no sentir tu partida
ya mi vida no era conocida

Te quiero papi, te extraño, te amo
Orgulloso de ser tu hiso, y a mí no me importa
yo soy tu hijo, y como tu hijo siempre te reclamo

TE AMO PAPI!!!

Papi.....Yuyo

Mi Abuelo, Mi viejo

Mi Abuelo, Mi viejo
Tu siempre decías que yo hera el negro que no cojia consejo

Si usted supiera, que yo siempre pienso en usted,
Dondequiera, su camino de buen hombre, yo seguiré

Yo siempre te quería mucho y nunca
pensé que te extrañaría tanto
siempre pienso en usted, orgulloso que usted era mi abuelo,
para el carajo, alto lo canto

uste vino a levantarme cuando estaba en coma
no se si era un sueño o no, pero me reganaste, gritaste que me
levantara y no jodiera, ahí me di de cuenta que no hera broma

un hombre de carácter fuerte, un hombre duro
como usted me decía, sique consejos negro, has
las cosas bien y tendrás un buen futuro

Te quiero abuelo, te extraño, nunca me di de cuenta
que uste era tan importante en mi vida
Un hombre serio, un hombre de familia, un hombre de
muchas lecciones, un hombre entero hasta su partida

Mi Abuelo, Mi viejo

The photos alone tell my story /
Las fotos cuentan mi historia

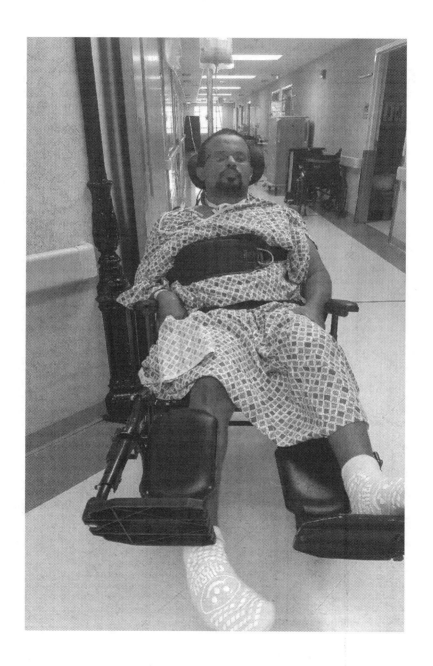

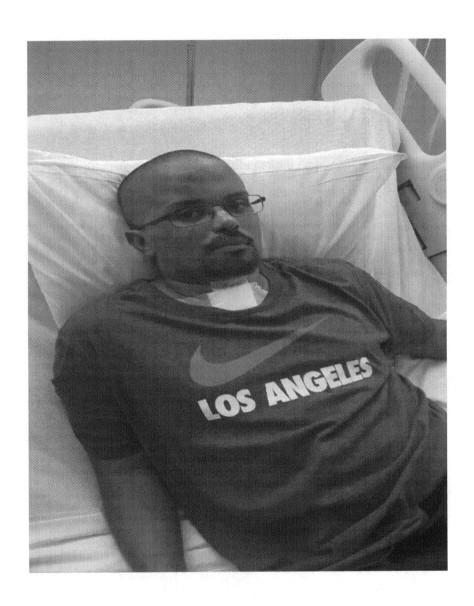

***OTHER BOOKS WRITTEN BY PEDRO LEBRON

-REBORN AT 36-

-THE HARD WAY UP-

SPANISH

-RENACIO A LOS 36-

-EL CAMINO DIFICIL HACIA ARRIBA-

Pedro Lebron
Rebornat36@gmail.com
www.rebornat36.com
www.renacioalos36.com (spanish)

Printed in the United States
By Bookmasters